For Once, Then, Nothing

For Once, Then, Nothing

Poems by

V. J. Saraf

With all best wishes

Cover design by Shay Culligan

ISBN: 978-1-954353-64-0

Kelsay Books
502 South 1040 East, A-119
American Fork, Utah, 84003

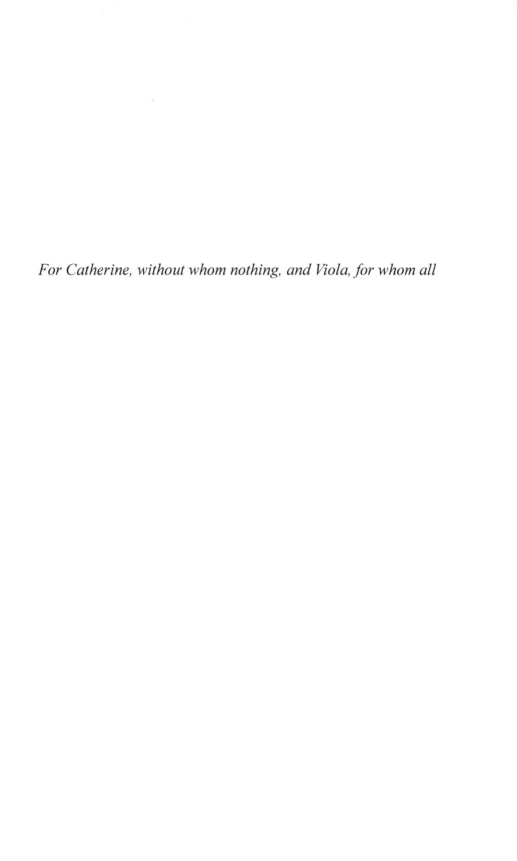

For Catherine, without whom nothing, and Viola, for whom all

Acknowledgments

The author's heartfelt thanks to Anton Yakovlev, *il miglior fabbro,* without whom this little book could not have come to be. Sincere thanks to the editors at Kelsay Books, for their generosity of spirit. Thanks to *The Ekphrastic Review,* for permitting republication of "Helen Sears." Thanks to J. G., and to Lucie Brock-Broido *in memoriam,* for kindness and guidance so long ago. With affection and gratitude to H. H., for opening the door to the king and the deer, for being the first to see and to say, and for continuing to see, long after. With affection to J. v. d. H., who was never too wise to wander through the castles in the air, and K. M., who refused and always refuses to let beautiful things go. With much gratitude to Profs. C. D., J. C., A. J., and others never known or no longer remembered who did what was hard, and kind, and not then clearly for the best, but which has turned out to have been for the best after all. With love and thanks to B. Z., who remains forever the path that led out of the forest. With love and thanks to A. S. and R. S., to whom the debt is infinite, and to L. S., who gave me song and all that comes with it. With thoughts of M., for what is most precious of all things. And above all, with love and gratitude to Catherine, *animae dimidium meae,* through whom alone I am more than a figment.

Time overtakes all
refusal to live,
makes men of those who would
remain merely figments.

The old tricks no longer seem
so funny;
time bestows tragedy
on what was once a private game.

Wisdom is thrust
upon the unwilling;
always just awakening
we remain always a step behind.

Thus, my friend, I too
have come to the place
where black rams are slaughtered,
staining ditches with their blood.

This time, I too see the hour and faces;
the smell of time around me
no longer seems
so benign.

—Apollodorus of Scyros

Contents

IV. Liana

V. Jerusalem

I. Emerald Lake

Old Friend

We've grown apart, the man I could have been
And who I am. He's like a neighboring train,
Parallel for a while, two feet away,
Seemingly headed to the same endpoint,

But lurching, suddenly, after some switch,
Off to the right, toward some distant hills,
Rapidly disappearing out of sight,
Leaving me to continue on alone.

We've grown apart, but I haven't forgot.
Sometimes in other men I'll catch a glimpse
Of what he looked like, and I feel refreshed,

As if a breeze blows through a field of corn:
The picker, burned and tired, will close his eyes.
It soothes him for a moment, then is gone.

Middle Age

A kangaroo hops through deserted dunes;
A knight swings freely down an empty board,
Chasing a lonely king; a penguin climbs
The coldest glacier on Antarctica,

Deracinated by the endless ice.
These days the middle of the board is thick
With pieces poised with crossfire, and the crush
Of wildebeests leaves no room to explore,

However deep the wanderlust. Each move
Is plotted fraught with foresight and long odds,
With actuarial splendor. And each move

The chance of victory, like a ghostly crown,
Glimmers clearer in darkness, and the deep
Catastrophe widens beneath your feet.

Lullaby

The bitterness is passed from hand to hand,
Father to son, mother to daughter, down
The stream of time that sprang from Adam's eyes

And Eve's lips when they left with scalded backs
And slept on cracked earth, shivering, like a prayer
That must not be forgotten, though the tongue

It came from is long dead: why do we shield
This little flame so carefully? No. Let
Magicians try to douse it, let explorers

Climb hand on hand up the sheer cliff to see
The traces of a garden long since burned
And indistinguishable from wild woods.

I gave up long ago. I only want
One glimpse of lilac from my bier of coals.

My Grey Gardens

Inside my heart there is a crumbling house,
Where raccoons wander freely, and the porch
Tilts over tangled masses of wild trees.
The sea howls mindless, echoing all night.

My grandfather retreated to this house,
When useful life was done, and never left.
My father, now, abandoned by his dreams,
Has taken over. I have hid there too,

For stretches of my life, but then the moon
Rising with strange light pulled me down the steps
And drew me back into the world. Still when
My life sinks low, I feel the urge again

And spend the night praying that you'll forgive
My silences, and block the tattered door.

Song: Across the Emerald Lake

Across the emerald lake, beyond the shore
Where golden birds flit between silver trees,
Beyond the ruby forest, where the moss
Shivers off hymns under the sapphire wind,

Up the steep slopes of chocolate mountain, where
Winged giraffes refresh themselves in pools
Of anise, where molasses chaparral
Secludes cocoons of giant butterflies,

There, in a palace made of pink brocade,
Guarded by inky clouds and Chinese lions,
On a stone bed beneath a counterpane
Of damask that the moon weaves out each night

Folded as thick as old sequoias' trunks,
There sleeps one moment unspoiled by unease.

Late Summer's Evening Walk

May the sky look like this the night I die:
Lavender with a smoke of stars and clouds,
Peaceful, unburdened by a sign of dread,
Expectant for tomorrow, fruitful day.

May students walk beside the lilac trees,
Falling in love, arguing over books
Just read and opening vistas which will take
Decades of life for them to understand.

May a small dog pee on a monument,
A mother push her stroller while the lamps
Flick on up Garden Street. May the moon leap,
Amber, then somersault across the night,

May breadtrucks then roll into Harvard Square,
And then the morning's first inbound Red Line.

Cardinal

I saw a cardinal flash past the road
In what was otherwise a gray, hard day.

Like a lit match, it made the bare trees glow
And crackle with a ritualistic flame.

Stopping to watch it as it flew by I
Thought of the human moments going on

Elsewhere: two people holding hands inside
A small café, a mother and her child

Cutting out gingerbread men, a brown dog
Licking a sleeping girl awake, in hope

Of a midmorning run; and then the flame
Thinned, as the cardinal flew far beyond

Some distant maples, and then died away,
Leaving me once more selfish in the frost.

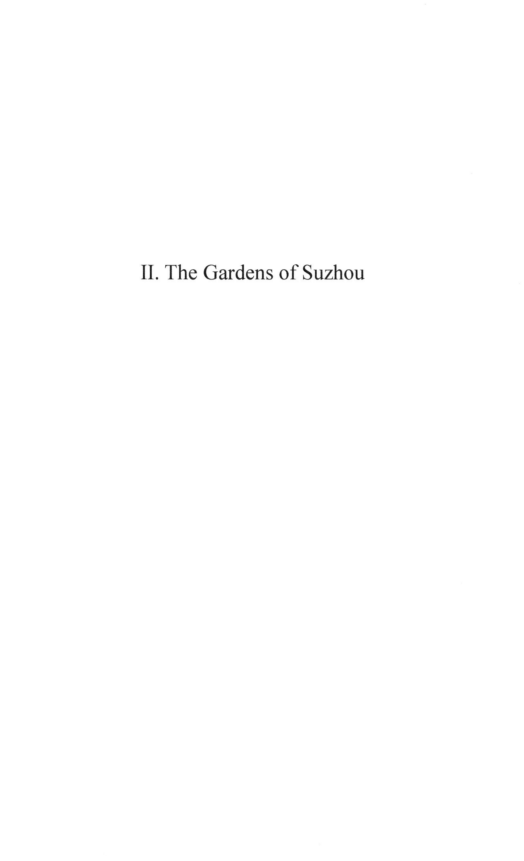

II. The Gardens of Suzhou

Goodbye, Café Algiers

History books, unread for decades, sag
The rosewood benchtops. Through a cloud of steam,
A waitress drops a pod of cardamom
In a brass pot of Turkish coffee. Near

A window, two young students read, their left
Hands overlapped, white earbuds in their ears.
A scribbling girl looks up and smiles at each
New guest who ducks beneath the trefoil screen

And settles on a stool. The light is dim
And somnolent; soft ghazals echo down
From somewhere in the wooden rafters. Thick
And wet, a spring snow falls outside for hours

Reflected in a mirror framed with pearl,
Near where I sit and sketch a tangerine.

At the Painted Burro

They ordered guacamole, a carafe
Of white sangria, and duck tacos. He
Was happy, quiet; she was talkative,

Affectionate. The waiter cleared their plates,
Brought mugs of hot spiced coffee. He sat still,
She spoke to him in measured words. His face

Turned red, and then the tears rolled from his eyes.
She held his hand, caressed it, looked at him
With caring that seemed genuine. He let

Her soothe him for a little longer, dried
His eyes off with his palms, and then they rose
And walked out slowly, his hand held in hers,

Her sad face filled with precious memories
That would soon be all that they would have shared.

Newport

There is no smell of rum around the docks
These days, not of starved bodies in the holds
Of moored ships. Narragansett Bay is flecked,
A sapphire set in diamonds, with white sails

Of pleasure sloops, heeling against the wind,
And bumptious herring gulls trying to split
Stuck clamshells on the tumbled rocks. But here,
Out on the cliff trail, none of this is seen:

Only wave after wave, dark green, explodes
Above the rocks as if some nemesis
Were reaching up its hand towards our necks,

Straining to clamber up to the thick brakes
And clifftop mansions, but could not quite reach
Its object, for at least another day.

Always Already (The Gardens of Suzhou)

Derrida, I imagine, could convince
Us that the garden came before the wild
Landscape we think it imitates. Suzhou
Would put you in that mind. When climbing up

Its bamboo-throttled labyrinths of rock
To spare pavilions overhanging ponds
Buggy with sweet osmanthus, watching drakes
Splash down and scatter orange carp, it comes

To you that all those Song and Yuan and Ming
Paintings, of plum trees, hermits, mountains, birds,
Were born in such pavilions, though we think
They framed the wildness of the world. Did those

Who made them, drunk on plum wine, even pine
To see the wild they felt nostalgic for?

Turnpike

It's victor's justice now. The neon lights,
Like flags of some superior alien race,
Flutter above the dutiful, dour streams
Of cars, their drivers shrouded in the black

Faceless dimension of similitude.
What do you love? The question flicks alive
In pale green dashboard lights. These souls like leaves
Blown down dry riverbeds, they blow away

This exit or the next, and merge back home,
Their circle of acknowledgment. But here
Each man or woman is just pounds of flesh
And metal, till the screeching of locked tires,

The crash of shattered glass, leaves them the crux
Of every passing driver's sudden care.

Friday Night at Amelia's

She walked into the restaurant with a smile,
Then kissed the object of it for a while,

And sat down, happy to be out with him.
But he'd been spoiling, and so now turned grim,

And let her have it for some petty crime
(She hadn't texted, or lost track of time

And showed up late, something like that). She blushed
With shock at first, but soon her face looked crushed,

As he went on. When he came to a stop,
They both sat quiet, stared at the tabletop.

Eventually, they held hands and he thought,
It seemed, *good, well, that lesson has been taught.*

But in her eyes I saw a lasting cost.
In his, an ignorance of what he'd lost.

Driving Home through Waltham

The orchards are long gone, cut for ski lifts
Then houses, but some apple trees still stand

On Prospect Hill, sheltering mockingbirds
And children flubbing cartwheels in the grass.

Somewhere in Washington a hand slams down
Upon a desk; a photograph is snapped.

In Pyongyang there is laughter; but in Seoul
Shivers. A bitter wind begins to blow

Across Japan, then onward to Juneau,
And down to North Dakota. Someone calls

In Minot for a dozen pizzas. Still,
The sun is bright on Prospect Hill, and no

One here can know whether some butterfly
In Kozelsk will uproot our last few trees.

For Once, Then, Nothing

A memory: late summer, bocce court
Behind a ranch house in Sebastopol.
An older colleague makes an errant throw;
The desert sun is sinking. Sipping wine,

I sat there quiet, feeling a stillness, some
Nothing-left-to-avoid I hadn't thought
Possible till that hour. Later that night,
Full moon, I drove along an empty road,

Top down, the scent of eucalyptus trees
Enveloping me through the highlands till
I reached the shore at Elk to spend the night.

At dawn, north to Fort Bragg. A contract signed,
Then back to Boston, and twelve years have passed;
I've never felt that evening lull again.

Commotion on Pearl Street

The #1 is coasting down Mass Ave
A half a block ahead of me. The wind
Is brisk, the temperature has dropped to five:
It's clear what I must do. I start to run,

A half-run, mostly, shuffling on the ice,
Hands alternating between swinging free
And being shoved in pockets. The real point
Is not so much to catch up to the bus,

Which is in fact too difficult. The point
Is to look so pathetic in my zeal
That when the driver checks the rear-view, she'll
Decide to pity me and wait too long

At the next stop. It works. I board relieved
And reacquire my air of dignity.

III. St. Anthony's Cave

Emmaus

There was a time when scotch and soda lit
Gas-jets beneath the day, which floated up
Above the date-palms and silk-cotton trees

That swirled through Poona, lurching up the Ghats,
And set a course toward the flawless moon
Making her way through thunderstorms to some

Parthenogenic tower, till sputtering flames
Dumped the dawn on the rooftop. Years passed by,
I came home, and became resigned to life

Of dirt and sweat. One day I sat to eat.
The bread was stale, the wine was sour. You cut
The heel off and caked it with cinnamon.

I looked into your face and knew the moon
Had grown tired of divinity at last.

Paraclausithyron

I don't know what to do so you can see
There is no me outside you anymore.

The sky, the trees, the snow upon the grass:
They have a name now, and the name is yours.

I can't look at things that look back at me.
I won't talk to things that will hear my words.

My guilt is in an unknown language. If
I prayed for shelter, to whom would I pray?

So take me as I am: a broken pot,
Though mended just enough to hold your wine,

So stars revolve upon your face all night.
I'm not one who can drink, but I can grasp,

And pass a steady night, knowing that we
Are what the Sufis sip from when they write.

At a University, Shanghai

Light rain falls quietly from the smoggy sky,
Sagging the plums and planes, while I sip tea
Brewed from chrysanthemums, under a stone
Arch of a stained and leaning portico

Designed by some impassioned Jesuit.
The talk is business, but my mind adrift,
Whether from jetlag or the atmosphere,
Is thinking of you as you used to be.

When was my first unkind word? Did I know
What I would lose? I see you as you smiled
Before we both became resilient.

I would unlearn that wisdom if I could,
Would go back to our Eden and stay there
With you, alone, as fickle as the rain.

Shantiniketan

Syrupy night air sways between the leaves
Of elms and lindens like the Gulf of Maine
Around moored ketches. *No one need mend nets
Nor hoist up traps today,* it seems to urge:

No one. I see Rabindranath at home,
Among his cane and peacocks, drink the old
Molten light of the setting sun through flutes;
I see him light an oil lamp and retire.

Gandhi turned earthquakes into strikes, but in
Bengal there was one place free of the Raj,
Floating in time like lotus-blossoms. Far

Away a siren breaks the silence, swells
Into a nasty bray outside my sill.
No man, I hear Donne say. *Ask not. For thee.*

Emergency Room, Mass General

Here is where there is something like a home
For those whom life is done with: those who sleep
In storefront doorways on a rainy night,
Those who have long since sold their hopes away

To fentanyl, and those whose minds grew snarled
Somewhere along the way. They get a cot,
An apple juice, a bit of chicken: more
Tenderness than they've seen since they were young.

Nurses check on them now and then. They moan
Because someone is listening. My wife
Is in a private room nearby, hooked up
To saline drips and monitors that flash

A soothing, steady symbol of her heart.
My hand is on her forehead in the dark.

Miscarriage

I woke this morning unconsoled to find
That snow had covered everything. The roads
Were empty: only church might draw cars out,
But it was just past dawn. High in the bare

Iced twigtops of an oak, a robin chipped,
Shuffling its feathers. Nothing else made noise,
Except a distant crack when, bent with drifts,
A cypress lost some branches. I lay still

In bed for hours, wishing that the snow
Would suffocate me too. And then a scrape,
Yankee and firm, came through the window. *So*

The churchgoers are up. Then more scrapes, and
I too rose then to dig my car out, glad
That after snow, there's always shoveling.

St. Anthony's Cave

If there were no flying demons with wide eyes
And needle noses, gouging at our skin,
No bloody froglike critters munching toes,
No princesses with coils instead of legs,

We could not know how much we love the light,
Through which we reach even as, beaten blue,
We die within our cave. We could not know
The pleasure of revival, the cool kiss

Of angels on our forehead, the loud voice
Announcing we have passed the test. Of course
In this life we have only the dark cave,
The flying monsters, only hungry frogs:

The kiss is just conjecture. (Well, the light.
We also have the sweetness of the light.)

Aposiopesis (Logan Airport)

Move left and right, people, part to the sides,
With your slow baggage-carts and your Rough Guides:

I'm sure you're lovely, but you're in the way!
Let me enlighten you. This is the day

My wife comes home from Annecy. Until
Her face appears, you may as well be still,

Like Tussaud figures, for all that I see
Any spark in you. She is every tree,

Every dawn, every dusk, all birds, all snows,
The purple mountains, cold lakes, and the rows

Of silver corn. She is the peace within,
The breath that made the universe begin.

Until she comes, the world is lifeless clay,
Absent—The needle drops! Life starts to play.

Blueberry-Picking

There is no bear to rob my pail, but still
The blueberry hills of Stockbridge lie apart
From all that crushes soul. In well-pruned rows,

Facing the mountains thick with spruce and birch,
Cleansed by the holy pivot of the sun
Towards the Housatonic, bushes bring

Their fruits to light without shame, hope, or fear.
Picking, I pause to watch two beetles mate
On a warm leaf, while others scrape and delve
The juiciest berries. Cedar waxwings lurk

Around the netting. One blue and gem-green
Dragonfly's tangled in the mesh above
My head, unable to cram through, or find
The gash he slipped in by. There's no escape.

Atonement

The gibbous moon is watching fireworks
Soar high above the esplanade. For once,
There's something from the world of man to see:

Rainfalls of burning gold, roseate bombs,
Inverted waterfalls of purple. Planes
Fly slowly just above like pensive bees

Encountering strange flowers. Bored, the moon
Tilts back now in her slow fall to her rest
In western lakes. The fireworks go on;

The ocean seethes with colors. Stars look down
Politely from their incandescent dome,
Surrounding me, surrounding everything

That's like me, and a sudden night wind threads
Through us and onward to the Milky Way.

IV. Liana

Inauguration Day, 2017

Don't wait for wild barbarians to appear,
Dyed head to toe with woad, shaking their swords,
And rushing towards the walls. Don't picture wolves
And lions reclaiming grasslands strewn with ruins,
Or forests shriveled up through fire and blight,
And blackened waters rotting with dead fish.

Rather, an aqueduct begins to slack,
And no one cares to patch the leaks. A road
Cracks apart under wheels and ice, but since
Ox-carts still trundle through, it's left in shards.
The theater closes due to lack of zeal
For festivals. There are still births and deaths,
And songs and torches, but no one recalls
What it was like to wish all things were new.

Eastern Cottontail (Old Burying Ground, Cambridge)

small knobby knoll tangle of crabgrass clutch
of dandelion and garlic come now come
no owls here where the upright stones the cool
black gate o come my kits zig-zag your way

like that the purple twilight is our time
hush now lie still be still to left up high
blue jay now over here these roots and bark
white bark don't stray so far white bark is good

why are there mounds so strange no beavers no
moles and no roots so peaceful solemn breeze
sounds from somewhere a distant weasel no
harm here my kits in this place where we live

tonight but soon you'll go where foxes roam
zig-zag to me listen more fast come home

For Hilda Clayton

A sudden flash, and instinct surges, routes
All blood and energy towards the mind
That processes some unforeseen events:

Gray rocks, the size of pancakes, smooth and round,
Suddenly floating in the air like tools
Bouncing in lunar orbit; a fierce wind

As brute upon her face as storm-force gales
But from no rational source; a flying man
With hands pressed on his eyes, as debris spills

Upward and outward, like a blossom. Then
The searing pain, like touch of ice; brief thought
At last of what is happening. Still, in

Her conscientiousness, without regret,
She snaps the image with a dying hand.

On Learning that Lech Walesa Was an Informer

To know that you will have your fingers crushed
And rectum pierced, nose shattered, shoulders snapped,
And still to do the thing for which these griefs
Will fall upon you, is no modest deed.

So what if when they've got you in their hands,
You bend a little, sensing there's a way
To spare yourself the horror? Who's to judge?
The courage was when you had made the choice.

Then, if you bide your time, and wait your chance
And when it comes, you seize it with full heart,
And throw the executioners in hell,

Are you not then an angel, even though
Your knees were broken once? Shall not your will
Be judged by what it does when it is well?

In a Green Shade

i. Steppe Grass

not for myself not myself not for me
white lake of sunlight purple thistle not
for me the dragonflies or me there is
no me or you except when there is wind

then all at once surrender come reindeer
come musk-ox I am not afraid nor me
nor us into the churning night the lake
of acid there is no pain we stand here

we here we this way ghosts of nutrients
evaporate into that churning lake
to fall as soil we fall as soil we live
tomorrow fresh and green beneath spring storms

we rise we are then we are there we roll
like waves through years we are not but we play

ii. Kentucky Coffeetree

Where has it gone, the woolly mastodon?
Where have the mammoths wandered? For so long
No one has chewed our pods. Have they moved on?
We have not seen them in so very long.

Each year we hang our seed-pods and we long
To see the mastodons. But they have gone.
Our thick pods fall and lie around the lawn,
Unloved by anyone. Well, once, not long,

The Pawnee boiled our seeds, and sang a song,
And drank our seeds, because it made them strong.
But they too now are gone! Do we belong?
It seems so strange to be here. Is it wrong?

At least the orioles still come here at dawn:
They sit here and they sing some kind of song.

iii. Liana

If I could just hold on (these lemurs leap
And swing as if I weren't living), if
I could just cup some drops of rain, if I
Could focus long enough to wrap around

That next branch with its blue leaves (I have looked
Up at it now for so long I could wish
To let go when sifakas munch my stems
And rip me from the bark), if I could catch

One stream of sunlight, just one drip, I could
(If these ants would just let me think) I could
Reach out, I could strain up with curling shoots,
I could break through, break free, could circle where

The bats soar in the moonlight, I could climb
And climb and twirl myself around the sun.

Martin McGuinness

There was no beauty, terrible or not,
After the blood of Bogside was washed clean,
Only cold calculation and cold rage:
Young soldiers executed from close range

With as much care as with which bills are dropped
Into a mailbox when one walks to work;
Or gunmen kicked and hooded, made to stand
On pointe for days until their hair turned white

And minds were mush; a shrieking, nude ballet
To slake a paratrooper's lust. Still you,
McGuiness, were not taken in by this:

You staged all this as prologue to a peace.
No doubt there'd be some beauty in that plan,
If it were you who'd made the sacrifice.

Remembering Duk Koo Kim

i.

This night is like a boxer on his stool
Moments before the round in which he's killed.

The Perseids flash and glide and disappear;
Cicadas ululate in emptiness.

The heat is done with its free solo climb;
It sleeps now on the long-awaited peak.

No one's awake. The night's a swimming pool
Lit from above, wavering for someone.

ii.

The boxer takes it all in: shouting crowds,
Spotlights, the ring girls holding up a sign,

The number that he knows will be his end.
He's pushed as far as human being can push,

And is at peace for once: he's made it to
His destination. And the bell is rung.

An Old Man in Naples

Sifting through oranges and cantaloupes, he tries to guess their ripeness from the sound or softness. *Ariel, what would you say*, he mutters, *of this one? Too soon? Well well, the baby will not notice, so long as I eat it when I give it to her*. As the light grows dim, he walks up torchlit streets, just an old man passing through busy crowds, cuts toward the palace through a back street, falls as some drunk staggers into him. Hot blood stains his silk shirt. He scrambles up and shouts: *I'll dredge my books up*—but it's just a threat; there's no vendetta for which he would miss the consolation of two juice-stained hands.

At the Berkshire Theatre Festival

I wore a suit; you wore Hawaiian shirts,
Which makes sense for a wedding held inside
A New Age bowling alley. We were friends;
That was the only link we had that day.

Years went by and I hired you. You came.
Something went wrong, to this day I can't say
Just what it was. I had to let you go.
Five years you've been a busted heirloom in

My mind, a lost book, till I saw your face
Tonight across the seats at summer stock.
Life is too complicated for my taste,
Ed. I prefer straight, simple things, like loons

In flight across a lake. But such as life
Is, we must live it and apologize.

For Lučić-Baroni, Upon Reaching a Grand Slam Semifinal after Twenty Years

It doesn't matter what will come of it.
Most likely, nothing. Like deep orange clouds
That close an overcast day, it will flare
Then flicker out. Or maybe something will:

The way magnolias sometimes bloom in fall,
Dropping their red seeds in soon-frosted soil.
But that is not the point. What matters is:
You kept a promise made when you were young.

What matters is: you came back to the path
Where once you turned aside, but this time, wise,
Took one step straight ahead. A small step, yes,

But leading onwards, and what matters is
That you continued what you started, and
Can end now at a seasonable time.

For Alan Kurdi

i.

I sense you in the edges of the sky,
As if it were your eyelid, closed upon
Me like a speck of dust to keep me with
Your body, though I know you lounge apart,

Aloof beneath your cobra, watching life
Before you with its fits and starts enact
The mathematics of your fancy, my
Whole life the merest ricochet of quarks.

For though I've had my share of suffering,
However many times I could have drowned
In darkness, something waved a torch for me

And led me out. But I can't help but think
Of little Alan, drowned in the cold sea,
And wondering if I've misunderstood.

ii.

If you don't drown with Alan, you will not
Swim far. If you aren't raped outside Sinjar
You can't be pure. If you give thanks for grace,
Crowned in the flickering mitre of sunlight,

You're blind. Oh poor friend, drink the sea in waves,
The poison then the nectar. As songbirds
Blew storm-crazed from New Guinea up the links
Of Indonesia, through the crowded steppes

And Africa, then back through Lake Louise,
Down to an Andean shade, and everywhere
Were painted by barbarity and scents
Around them, distant jungle rains will drug

You when the desert tortures, and when fruits
Ripen for you, you will starve for the dead.

V. Jerusalem

Mrs. Fiske Warren and Her Daughter Rachel

Mrs. Fiske Warren stares with confidence
At Sargent, while he paints. And why not? She's
At peace here in the Gardners' Gothic Room,
Her proud flushed face tamed by a light pink dress

By choice. (She once turned down a teaching post
At Radcliffe.) But her daughter Rachel, twelve,
Is lost in thought, unwilling to submit
To what the painter wants. We know that she

Will dig for ruins in Guatemala, spy
In Costa Rica for the Navy, spend
Old age with Irish freedom-fighters. He
Can't know this yet; but Sargent sees that though

Her head leans on her mother's shoulder, there's
No comfort for her in her mother's choice.

Angel

It makes no difference to me where I'm sent—
To this red star, awakening fresh blue rain
From mists of electricity that sparked
A billion years before I came; to where

The edge encounters absence and must take
The form my fingers shape in symmetries;
To where, upon a mountain ringed by sea,
Breath of resolve blows through the mind of man

Looking out on an emptiness. It makes
No difference, no, I carry out the plan
To all things equally, with wonderment

At what I land upon: world after world,
A cosmic garden always coming in
To bloom, through me: the signal in the soil.

Persepolis

Was it for the lost smells of Babylon,
The temple incense mixed with flowering quince,
Redolent of the Earth's genetic dream:

An undivided garden? Or the swarm,
Frantic and stinging, of rebellious kings
Cloaking themselves in monsoons and gold coins

Beyond the reach of armies? Or the lions
That still paced at Persepolis, royal blue,
Judgmental in their silence? These perhaps,

Or something else. All that we know is when
He could have stopped, grown old in palaces
From Samarkand to Balkh, Antiochus

Like a blue jay toward a sleeping hawk
Too near his nest, rushed to Thermopylae.

Rimbaud in Abyssinia

I don't know what you're speaking of. *Voyelles?*
I can't be bothered with such decadence.
Words are for taking stock of ivory,
Rifles, and damask, or reconnaissance

Out of the hinterlands for my friend Ilg.
Listen, you are mistaken. He who wrote
Le Bateau Ivre was a deranged child.
Perhaps that was his truth. But as you see

My truth is money. And a lot of risk:
I do acknowledge that. My caravans
Go deeper in the jungle and come back
Heavier with rare cargo than the rest:

That's all the genius that I possess.
Here in Harar, my poetry is life.

Uplistsikhe, Georgia (Encounter with the Argonauts)

Most likely they were cooking mutton on
A spit, or burning goat's fat to the sky,
Or hauling water from the Kura in
Bronze urns painstakingly up the sharp rocks.

They saw a strange sight: gleaming from afar,
A hundred men making their way along
The river to a mountain pass. The chief
Sent his son to inquire what thing they sought.

All stood still till he came back with the news:
A golden fleece. Then laughter, more amazed
Than dubious. Give them some meat and wine,
The chief said. It was done. The men moved on,

And everyone got back to the day's tasks,
With one new story now to tell the young.

Missing Link (The Mind of a Mandrill)

The thing is, if you will indulge me, that
We must keep to the main point, mustn't let
Ourselves become distracted. That is why,
If you'll permit me, I must concentrate

Upon your face a little longer, must
Discern, deduce (don't be distracted if
I stroke my chin: it helps the thinking), must
Place you. The thing is, if you will indulge,

We must keep to the main thing, and the truth
Is that among so many palm trees, swaying
And fruitful, with you here, we must not let
Ourselves become dull, like the leopards, must

Stay true to meditation on the main
Thrust, which is wonderful; and I must go.

Peter Basile

No one was more shocked than Peter himself.
Just moments earlier, he'd been a clown,
Waving a frying pan like a flag above
The walls, and shooting arrows randomly.

But suddenly, Richard the Lionheart,
Walking back to his tent outside the gate,
Fell bleeding from the neck. The wound was deep
And gangrenous. His council vowed revenge,

But he himself, who'd ordered massacres
At Arsuf and at Acre with no remorse,
Seemed to find mercy as he died, and begged
His men to set the jester free. But they

Were too steeped in his way of life to heed
His prayers. Basile was flayed alive, then burned.

On a Photo of Marilyn Monroe

The greatest fantasy is not the look
That says *I want you, honey.* No, it's plain
That is in fact what she is smiling out,
Blonde and rose-nippled on her scarlet throw.

The fantasy is that she *likes* this look,
It flows spontaneously from her warm heart,
And from her opposition to the shame
That's locked up self-expression until now.

The fantasy is what we tell ourselves
About the way this glossy page was made:
The gaffers and the best boys laugh and smoke,
Then she walks in, sets down her tea, disrobes,

And awes them out of their misogyny,
Then dresses and strides out, sipping her tea.

Jerusalem

Pontius, though he'd spent his dusty days
In crop disputes, taxes, and road repairs,
Had read his Plato, knew how Socrates
Drank hemlock to make sure his wisdom lived

When just one plea would have spared him from death;
And knew Achilles' choice, though it bereaved
His mother, to be worth long memory
In lieu of long life. So, although he was,

Josephus writes, cruel, haughty, and unmoved
By Jewish mysticism, when that one man,
Though Jewish, stood before him in a guise

He understood, he trembled at the brush
Of something, for one instant, greater than
The dust, and let the young man have his wish.

Helen Sears

There's something missing: little Helen Sears,
In white dress and white shoes, standing between
The room's red darkness and the green-gold light
Exploding through a window on the blue

Hydrangeas in their brass urns, glowing up
Over her face like revelation, seems
Unaware of the flowers her fingers touch.
Empty some call her, thinking Sargent viewed

Her as a kind of pretty object. But
Look close: her right leg's crossed over the left
Completely, as if in ecstatic dance.
Her fingers, arched, are playing the petals like

Piano keys. Her stern eyes stare outside,
At what she's missing so the man can paint.

Ballad of the *Sea Nymph*

Idiots. What else can I really say?
One of them'd never sailed before, while mine
Who had sailed seemed to go to pieces. Why
Didn't we pull in at the island ports

We passed while we were drifting? Why not try
To turn the cooking fuel-packs into flares?
Why not try something, at least? But no. Day
On day, we drifted aimlessly. We ate

(Quite well, that was the strange thing), and we slept,
And went for brief walks up and down the boat,
And did our thing over the edge, and sang

(The people did, we barked in time) and there
Was no sense of a panic, we were all
Quite happy drifting nowhere. Idiots.

ii.

Still, it was peaceful. That much must be said.
The sea, electric in the moonlight, hummed
Louder each night and overwhelmed our brains:
We'd lie there, silently, watching the whales

Crest momentarily, quite far away,
Then disappear, like fragments of some truth
Trying to blossom in our solitude
But not quite finding us rich soil enough.

That was disheartening. But it was nice,
For once, that something, someone, thought we might
Be a good vessel for its mysteries,

Being as how on land we mostly sleep
And beg for rubs and eat. Although we failed,
I'm not sure that it wasn't grand to try.

iii.

It did get boring at some point. You'd watch
The moon night after night: at first it seemed
To have something to say but pitched so high
Your ears could not quite catch it, and you'd strain

Everything in your body, from your gut
Up to your throat to try to resonate
With its shrill, blinkless message. But no luck.
Eventually, we started to suspect

The moon was just a moon, the waves were just
Dangerous, filled with sharks, and salt, and worse,
And we were just ridiculous, a raft

Of hobos, sailing toward the stars but bound
To end up on some Chinese fishing boat,
Wrapped up in blankets, glum and mortified.

iv.

When we got back to land, the questions! God.
Why did you not . . . When last . . . What was the thought . . .
As if this was the point! Don't get me wrong,
I was quite happy back on solid ground,

Chasing the squirrels, sunning on the couch,
And whatnot. After months of sitting still,
With cabin fever, I was so relieved
To have my freedom back! And yet the goal

Wasn't to get somewhere, not really, so
There's no point in inspecting all our logs,
Our charts, and so on. What it was, you see,

Was that for so long as we weren't found
We had no choices, made no conscious moves;
We just bore witness to the gorgeous world:

v.

The crazy world: meteors blazed all night,
Rainclouds rolled from infinity and dragged
A curtain over everything, then left
The waters clear and seething with bright fish;

The rising sun, washing the atmosphere
With one more day's salvation; and the winds
Relentless like wild horses: I assert
I know them with minuteness, how they taste,

Or smell, or make you feel. Here, in the yard,
You put your faith in things you like to do.
But I have seen so much that dwarfs our reach,
And that's my pride. When I've been put to sleep,

Tell them I said I knew what it was worth,
This world, though I can't tell you what it is.

Dark Energy

Eternity and then this passing light,
Burning rose on its parabolic plane,
Its shivers imperceptible, the strain
Of distant white collapses on its flight.

This passing light, and then eternity,
Except somewhere its nucleus congeals
Harvesting spin, and silently reveals
How here a charge must flicker and break free

And spawn like blossoms through an organon
Infinitudes of cosmic progeny,
Refractions to flood over the bare tree
Of this one universe, and moving on

Must leave me as a multitude until
Time's axiom collapses and is still.

Morning Raga

As he sits still bare-chested on the dirt, eyes closed but tensely as the dawn bleeds out of night, light winds shrill through the banyan leaves like restless sleepers. Then the sun leaps clear, shouts color into everything: the trees, the huts, the river; which, throbbing to life, still glisten with the memory of the womb of shadow they till recently were in and will return to when the sun has set. There is nobody for a dozen miles and God is far more distant, so he sings a single, raspy *sa,* then as always, rises to milk the cows. One word, he knows, is either nothing, or else everything.

About the Author

V. J. Saraf lives in Cambridge, Massachusetts, with his wife and daughter. Born and raised in Virginia, he studied classics and physics at Harvard University and has lived previously in Germany and India. He runs a medical software and publishing business headquartered in Waltham, Massachusetts, and writes poetry on weekends. He enjoys sailing among the Harbor Islands in Boston Harbor, sketching in the few remaining cafés of Harvard Square, and passing summer nights watching the Red Sox at Fenway Park.